What Would You Do in a
Library?

Susan Kralovansky

Consulting Editor, Diane Craig, M.A./Reading Specialist

A Division of ABDO

ABDO
Publishing Company

visit us at www.abdopublishing.com

Published by ABDO Publishing Company, a division of ABDO, P.O. Box 398166, Minneapolis, Minnesota 55439. Copyright © 2013 by Abdo Consulting Group, Inc. International copyrights reserved in all countries. No part of this book may be reproduced in any form without written permission from the publisher. Super SandCastle™ is a trademark and logo of ABDO Publishing Company.

Printed in the United States of America, North Mankato, Minnesota
102012
012013

 PRINTED ON RECYCLED PAPER

Editor: Liz Salzmann
Content Developer: Nancy Tuminelly
Cover and Interior Design and Production: Kelly Doudna, Mighty Media, Inc.
Photo Credits: Kelly Doudna, Shutterstock
Online Card Catalog: Hennepin County Library

Library of Congress Cataloging-in-Publication Data

Kralovansky, Susan.
 What would you do in a library? / Susan Kralovansky.
   p. cm. -- (Library resources)
ISBN 978-1-61783-602-2
1. Libraries--Juvenile literature. I. Title.
027--dc15

2012946822

Super SandCastle™ books are created by a team of professional educators, reading specialists, and content developers around five essential components—phonemic awareness, phonics, vocabulary, text comprehension, and fluency—to assist young readers as they develop reading skills and strategies and increase their general knowledge. All books are written, reviewed, and leveled for guided reading, early reading intervention, and Accelerated Reader® programs for use in shared, guided, and independent reading and writing activities to support a balanced approach to literacy instruction.

Contents

What would you do
if you were in a library?

Every
library has
a librarian. The
librarian knows
everything!

4

PUBLIC LIBRARY

Ms. Watson
LIBRARIAN

A librarian takes care of thousands of books.

The Library of Congress in Washington, D.C., has more than 22 million books.

A library has picture books, chapter books, encyclopedias, dictionaries, atlases, and more!

7

The librarian can help you find the perfect book. Just ask for what you want.

Hey, Librarian! Do you have any snake books?

Do you have a drawing book?

Picture books and chapter books are made–up stories. They are fiction books.

Tina Turtle Takes the Train

10

Dear Librarian,

Thanks for the book about Tina Turtle. I have a pet turtle, so it was fun reading a story about one. It is my favorite book ever!

From a turtle lover and your biggest fan.

Other books are about real people, places, and things. They are nonfiction books.

 There are ten main groups of nonfiction books.

There are several ways to find a book. You can look on the shelves. You can use the catalog. You can ask a librarian for help.

A catalog used to be a set of drawers filled with paper cards. Today it is usually on a computer.

Fiction books are arranged by the authors' last names. Sometimes they are also grouped by type of fiction.

 Some types of fiction are picture books, mysteries, science fiction, and general fiction.

Dear Librarian,

Thanks for the cool science fiction book! It is a great story about traveling in space.

Now I know where to find more books by the same author.

From your local space nut.

17

Nonfiction books have call numbers. Each book has its own number. It tells you where in the library the book is kept.

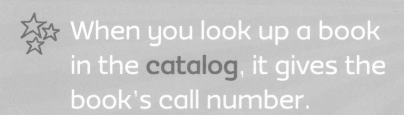

When you look up a book in the catalog, it gives the book's call number.

The call number is also on the book's spine.

There are two main call number systems. They are the Dewey Decimal Classification and the Library of Congress Classification.

The Library of Congress Classification is used mainly in academic libraries.

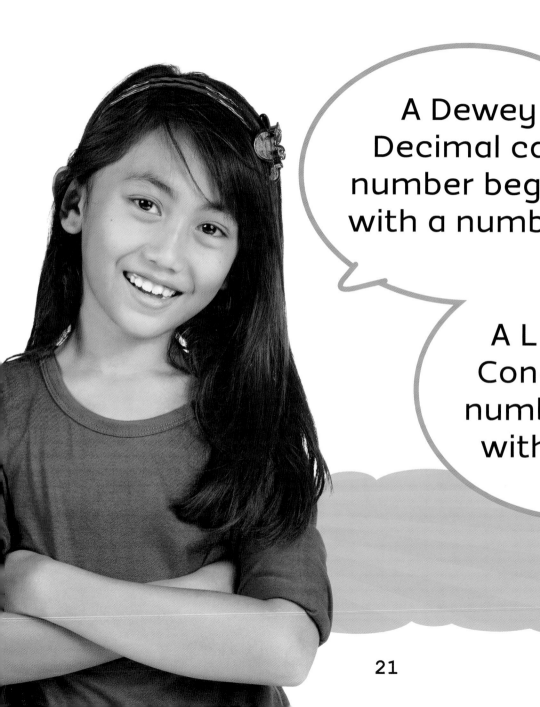

A Dewey Decimal call number begins with a number.

A Library of Congress call number begins with a letter.

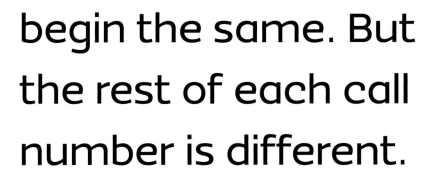

Nonfiction books are grouped by subject. Books on the same subject have call numbers that begin the same. But the rest of each call number is different.

Hola,

I am learning Spanish.
I know where to find
Spanish books at the library.

Their call numbers start
with 460 through 468.

From your muy favorite
Spanish-speaking kid.

After you find a book, you can read it at the library. Or you can check the book out and take it home.

 Ask the librarian how you can get your own library card.

There are more than just books at the library.

I read my favorite magazines at the library. It has newspapers too.

My library has author visits, storytellers, and book parties.

27

29

You'll find a lot of fun things to read and do at the library. There are great books and a lot more. Just ask the librarian!

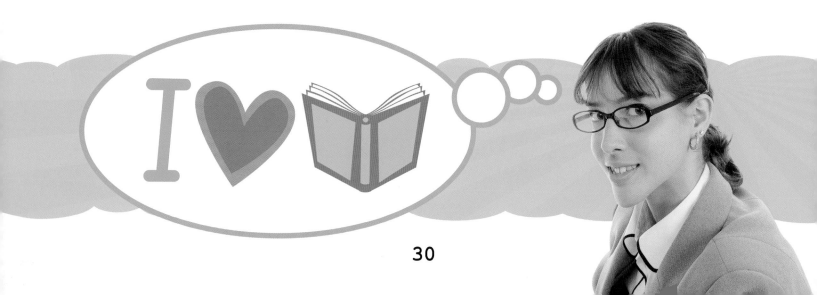

Glossary

academic – having to do with a college or university.

atlas – a book of maps.

catalog – a list of all the books, magazines, CDs, and DVDs in a library.

dictionary – a book that lists words and their meanings.

drawer – a sliding box that can be pulled out of a piece of furniture.

encyclopedia – a book or set of books with information arranged alphabetically by subject.

shelf – a thin, flat surface used to store things.

spine – the part of a book cover where the pages are attached.